super word search puzzles for kids

Official Mensa
Puzzle Book

John Chaneski

Sterling Publishing Co., Inc.
NEW YORK

For Jennifer. Sometimes I just can't find the words.

Edited by Peter Gordon

12   14   16   18   20   19   17   15   13   11

Published by Sterling Publishing Co., Inc.
387 Park Avenue South, New York, NY 10016
© 2001 by John Chaneski
Distributed in Canada by Sterling Publishing
c/o Canadian Manda Group, 165 Dufferin Street
Toronto, Ontario, Canada M6K 3H6
Distributed in Great Britain and Europe by Chris Lloyd at Orca Book
Services, Stanley House, Fleets Lane, Poole BH15 3AJ, England
Distributed in Australia by Capricorn Link (Australia) Pty. Ltd.
P.O. Box 704, Windsor, NSW 2756, Australia

Sterling ISBN-13: 978-0-8069-4417-3
ISBN-10: 0-8069-4417-X

For information about custom editions, special sales, premium and
corporate purchases, please contact Sterling Special Sales
Department at 800-805-5489 or specialsales@sterlingpub.com.

Contents

Introduction

Congratulations! By selecting this book you've shown great intelligence (and great taste). Scientists believe that the brain is like a muscle: mental exercise, like puzzle-solving, keeps the mind flexible, keen, and strong. Plus, puzzles are a lot more interesting than lifting heavy objects over and over. Word searches are an excellent "gateway" that prepares you for crosswords, double crostics, cryptograms, and an entire universe of fun.

Here are some directions to help you in solving word searches. Each puzzle consists of a letter grid and a word list. Each of the twenty or so words or phrases in a list can be found somewhere in the letter grid above it. The words are always in a straight line, but they can appear reading forward, backward, up, down, or diagonally. Diagonal words might read in any one of the four diagonal directions.

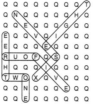

ONE is down, TWO is across, THREE is up, FOUR is backward, FIVE is down-right, SIX is down-left, SEVEN is up-left, and EIGHT is up-right. Right? So there are eight possible directions in all, and this is our promise to you: Each puzzle in this book uses all eight directions! No direction is left unused! And you'll notice that several letters are used in more than one word, and that all the words are connected. Aren't you impressed? Also, remember that all spaces and punctuation are ignored, so the phrase "Who's the boss, Ross?" would appear in the grid, in some direction, as WHOSTHEBOSSROSS.

You can work a word search in any of a dozen different ways. You can search for across words first; you can search for down words first; you can search for words with unusual letters in them, like Q, Z, X, or J; you can skip around different parts of the grid; you can work your way methodically from top to bottom; or you can stand on your head and yell at the puzzle, "WHO'S THE BOSS, ROSS?" but, of course, people will stare at you.

When you have found a word, you can draw a loop around it, circle each letter, draw a line through it, whatever you like. It's also a good idea to cross the words off the list as you find them, as a reminder.

The 56 puzzles in this book all have different themes (okay, "Actors" and "Actresses" aren't that different—you got me). Solve them in order or skip around. Here's a tip: Most of the grids are rectangular, with 11 letters across and 15 down. So, if a word is 12 letters long, it must be either up or down.

Some grids have unusual shapes that relate to their themes and some of them require you to guess the theme. You can spot these by the fact that they don't have a word list (and they say "Guess the Theme" at the top). We've given you the first letter of each grid entry and a blank for every other letter in the word. Use these to find a few words and then guess the theme to help you find the rest. If you get stumped, the full word lists are on pages 63 and 64.

If you've circled all the words and phrases hidden in a grid, you'll find that the unused letters, read in order line by line, will spell out a hidden message! Spooky, huh? The message will be a riddle, quotation, definition, joke, or some other information related to the puzzle's theme, but you'll have to figure out where the spaces go and what punctuation is used on your own.

If you come across a word or phrase you've never heard of before, go on and look it up. It will surely be useful to you some-day. And speaking of useful, here's an idea: Puzzles make great gifts or favors. Carefully cut out the "Happy Birthday!" word search and give it to a cousin for his or her birthday, or give Mom the "Valentine's Day" puzzle for Valentine's Day!

I just want to let you know one more thing: Puzzles can be just as fun to create as they are to solve. When you've finished this book, why not give it a try? In the meantime, you've got words to find, so get out there and have fun!　　　—John Chaneski

Guess the Theme Instructions

Five of the puzzles in this book do not include word lists. Instead, below the grid there are blanks that need to be filled in. In puzzle 31, clues are given as in a crossword, and you need to answer the clues to determine the words. If you find a word in the grid, look through the clues to find which one matches it. The other four puzzles are "Guess the Theme." In these, you need to find the words on your own and determine what they have in common. The initial letters are given and the words appear in alphabetical order (except in puzzle 44, in which the words are in a particular order that you have to determine). For example, if the item were APPLE TREE, the blanks would show A _ _ _ _ _ _ _ _ . If you find a word that doesn't fit any of the blanks, ignore it, since it's not part of the puzzle. If you need help, the words to be found appear on pages 63 and 64.

When you're finished looping, the unused letters read row by row from top to bottom will spell out a message that reveals the puzzle's theme.

1. SOUND OFF!

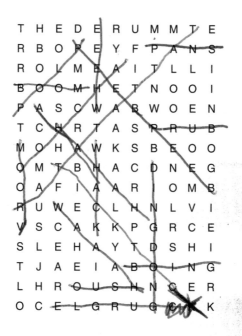

```
T  H  E  D  E  R  U  M  M  T  E
R  B  O  R  E  Y  F  P  A  N  S
R  O  L  M  E  A  I  T  L  L  I
B  O  O  M  H  E  T  N  O  O  I
P  A  S  C  W  A  B  W  O  E  N
T  C  H  R  T  A  S  P  R  U  B
M  O  H  A  W  K  S  B  E  O  O
O  M  T  B  H  A  C  D  N  E  G
O  A  F  I  A  A  R  I  O  M  B
R  U  W  E  C  L  H  N  L  V  I
V  S  C  A  K  K  P  G  R  C  E
S  L  E  H  A  Y  T  D  S  H  I
T  J  A  E  I  A  B  O  I  N  G
L  H  R  O  U  S  H  N  C  E  R
O  C  E  L  G  R  U  G  C  K  K
```

AHCHOO ✓	OOPS ✓
BEEP BEEP ✓	OUCH ✓
BOING ✓	PLOP ✓ ✓
BOOM ✓	RAT-A-TAT-TAT
BURP ✓	SNAP ✓
CLICK	TICKTOCK ✓
CREAK	VROOM ✓
DING-DONG ✓	WAAAH ✓✓
GURGLE ✓	WHACK ✓
HA HA HA ✓	WHEEE ✓

2. UP AND DOWN, BACK AND FORTH

```
B  A  D  S  G  N  I  W  S  S  W
W  K  T  R  A  P  E  Z  E  A  R
E  O  A  D  O  O  M  T  V  O  R
B  P  R  A  L  W  L  E  T  B  E
H  A  A  D  S  I  S  A  C  R  T
G  L  T  S  S  T  V  S  U  H  S
N  I  E  A  R  E  T  T  O  S  A
O  N  N  S  L  E  A  T  H  R  O
P  D  N  E  C  R  P  R  E  W  C
G  R  I  A  E  A  Y  P  C  T  R
N  O  S  P  H  S  L  L  I  H  E
I  M  M  E  B  A  L  A  L  Z  L
P  E  N  D  U  L  U  M  T  B  L
T  O  U  N  C  E  Y  O  Y  O  O
S  H  I  K  E  R  E  K  C  O  R
```

CROSSWORD	ROCKER
ELEVATOR	ROLLER COASTER
ESCALATOR	SWINGS
GRAPH	TEMPERATURE
HIKER	TENNIS
HILLS	TRAPEZE
MOOD	WAVES
PALINDROME	WORD SEARCH
PENDULUM	YO-YO
PING-PONG	ZIPPER

3. POP CHARTS 2001

```
M  P  K  C  O  R  D  I  K  E  I
C  A  U  Q  M  N  T  M  C  A  S
D  C  S  F  R  E  A  R  Y  T  Y
E  I  H  A  F  C  N  E  N  T  O
S  U  N  R  Y  D  R  I  D  E  B
T  Z  I  G  I  D  A  A  M  N  T
I  Y  R  A  R  S  N  D  A  E  E
N  A  B  D  L  G  T  U  D  C  E
Y  J  A  L  E  M  K  I  O  Y  R
S  E  A  L  I  H  T  W  N  I  T
C  T  O  K  I  M  C  S  N  A  S
H  H  L  T  A  Y  Y  T  A  W  K
I  I  O  E  H  N  A  A  I  N  C
L  D  R  I  C  K  Y  H  L  W  A
D  D  E  S  Y  E  N  T  I  R  B
```

AALIYAH	EMINEM
ALL SAINTS	JAY-Z
BACKSTREET BOYS	KID ROCK
BRITNEY	LIL' KIM
B*WITCHED	MACY GRAY
CHRISTINA	MADONNA
D'ANGELO	'N SYNC
DESTINY'S CHILD	PUFF DADDY
DR. DRE	RICKY
DREAM	SISQÓ

4. 21 MOST COMMON LAST NAMES

Below is a list of 20 of the 21 most common last names in the United States. You'll notice that one is missing. Solve the puzzle to find out why.

```
N  G  A  N  O  S  P  M  O  H  T
W  M  A  E  O  M  N  U  Z  M  B
H  A  R  R  I  S  E  E  R  S  S
I  I  X  L  C  H  N  T  E  A  E
T  N  L  M  T  I  A  I  M  R  T
E  E  S  I  T  I  A  O  B  M  N
R  I  M  R  J  O  H  N  S  O  N
S  S  A  F  O  T  D  U  N  O  R
D  M  I  N  A  K  I  A  S  R  N
N  S  L  Y  D  I  R  K  V  E  W
W  D  L  E  N  E  C  A  A  I  M
O  O  I  E  N  A  R  U  L  M  S
R  B  W  E  J  R  N  S  I  C  N
B  E  T  S  E  N  O  J  O  E  E
N  M  A  R  T  N  I  N  E  N  Z
```

1. SMITH	11. ANDERSON
2. JOHNSON	12. THOMAS
3. WILLIAMS	13. JACKSON
4. JONES	14. WHITE
5. BROWN	15. HARRIS
6. DAVIS	17. THOMPSON
7. MILLER	18. GARCIA
8. WILSON	19. MARTINEZ
9. MOORE	20. ROBINSON
10. TAYLOR	21. CLARK

5. HARRY POTTER

```
H  A  R  E  N  O  I  M  R  E  H
R  Y  S  L  Y  T  H  E  R  I  N
G  S  T  R  A  W  G  O  H  P  Q
O  R  T  T  Y  E  D  R  B  U  O
T  O  Y  L  L  E  P  S  I  K  S
R  K  A  F  L  R  L  D  C  E  P
O  U  C  B  F  B  D  S  W  A  L
M  I  M  I  D  I  R  G  A  H  R
E  U  S  H  T  N  N  E  N  E  D
D  I  G  C  O  S  N  D  D  A  W
L  R  H  G  W  B  M  O  O  U  T
O  C  A  U  L  D  R  O  N  R  F
V  R  O  Z  S  E  G  H  O  S  T
D  R  T  Y  I  L  S  A  N  R  G
U  A  G  E  S  W  I  T  C  H  B
```

BROOMSTICK	OWLS
CAULDRON	QUIDDITCH
DRAGON	SCAR
DUMBLEDORE	SLYTHERIN
GHOST	SPELL
GRYFFINDOR	VOLDEMORT
HAGRID	WAND
HERMIONE	WEASLEY
HOGWARTS	WITCH
MUGGLES	WIZARD

6. CLASSIC TOYS

```
L  T  O  P  O  O  H  A  L  U  H
I  Y  E  S  T  O  T  E  R  S  Y
N  F  E  E  A  T  E  O  L  U  E
C  R  E  E  B  H  S  I  P  T  A
O  Y  O  Y  W  S  N  D  C  S  S
L  T  J  G  D  K  I  H  O  N  Y
N  R  I  I  Y  C  A  R  K  S  B
L  B  G  N  L  S  R  E  F  K  A
O  T  O  N  K  A  T  R  U  C  K
G  S  E  E  A  E  S  M  L  A  E
S  R  T  R  I  P  R  O  E  J  O
F  C  T  B  A  T  O  T  G  H  V
H  E  R  P  L  A  Y  D  O  H  E
M  A  R  B  L  E  S  A  D  Y  N
B  Y  T  T  U  P  Y  L  L  I  S
```

BARBIE	MARBLES
BIG WHEEL	NERF
EASY-BAKE OVEN	PLAY-DOH
ETCH A SKETCH	SILLY PUTTY
FRISBEE	SLINKY
G.I. JOE	TINKERTOYS
HULA-HOOP	TONKA TRUCK
JACKS	TOPS
LEGO	TRAIN SET
LINCOLN LOGS	YO-YO

7. "RUN ___"

```
A  G  O  O  T  H  R  O  U  G  H
D  D  I  C  T  T  I  T  O  L  N
Y  A  W  A  A  R  O  N  L  Y  D
W  I  L  S  G  S  L  I  D  H  N
F  A  V  H  S  A  M  L  R  E  U
L  O  W  O  N  E  I  W  E  L  O
L  O  R  R  H  W  V  N  E  N  R
R  C  A  T  C  H  K  I  S  S  A
A  R  F  O  H  N  E  E  H  T  S
D  O  E  U  N  E  N  D  R  A  G
E  O  E  V  D  T  R  D  L  E  N
G  F  W  D  E  E  S  O  T  I  I
G  N  I  N  T  F  N  I  S  O  R
A  N  C  S  F  G  A  O  R  E  R
R  E  V  O  C  R  O  F  U  N  S
```

ACROSS	LOW ON
A FEVER	OF THE MILL
AGAINST	-ON SENTENCE
ALONG	RAGGED
AWAY	RINGS AROUND
-CATCH-KISS	RIOT
DOWN	SHORT
FOR COVER	THROUGH
FOR THE ROSES	TO SEED
INTO	WILD

8. POKÉMON

```
        O  N  I  X  P  B
     I  W  U  P  I  R  O  B
     L  L  T  I  D  O  E  U  N  R
  R  A  V  K  Y  T  O  L  E  L  Y  A
D  C  E  A  R  L  O  B  D  I  S  S  T  M
T  I  C  D  O  T  A  H  E  E  W  S  A  A
L  H  G  V  N  S        E  A  Q  A  N  C
U  N  A  L  A  A        W  U  D  S  G  H
E  A  B  U  E  G  M  R  I  C  H  N  E  O
I  N  R  G  S  T  A  R  Y  U  I  F  L  P
  R  A  T  T  A  T  A  A  F  A  R  A
     X  I  P  L  U  V  F  H  A  N
     E  E  Z  W  O  R  D  C
     D  W  K  I  D  E
```

ABRA	PIKACHU
BULBASAUR	POLIWAG
CHARMANDER	PONYTA
DIGLETT	RATTATA
DODUO	SQUIRTLE
DROWZEE	STARYU
GASTLY	TANGELA
KOFFING	VOLTORB
MACHOP	VULPIX
ONIX	WEEDLE

9. BOXING MATCH

Each entry in the list contains the word BOX, but in the grid, every BOX appears as a ■ symbol. For example, if SKYBOX were in the list, it would appear in the grid as SKY■.

```
■  L  ■  Y  T  L  A  N  E  P  S  I  F
E  R  W  I  ■  T  O  L  L  A  B  ■  S
M  L  O  I  K  R  E  A  N  B  T  E  O
A  X  D  O  O  F  E  D  C  I  H  H  O
T  W  N  C  P  O  ■  T  S  L  A  T  T
C  ■  I  E  S  L  Y  O  T  O  U  N  N
H  S  W  T  O  E  P  V  ■  A  E  I  R
■  S  O  O  N  E  K  N  J  L  H  K  O
W  E  T  A  D  E  W  M  U  S  I  C  ■
H  R  C  E  P  A  S  A  K  T  Y  A  O
U  P  F  I  A  ■  H  S  E  R  E  J  M
P  A  N  D  O  R  A  S  ■  G  O  I  N
S  G  T  ■  E  V  O  L  G  O  G  E  T
```

BALLOT BOX	POOR BOX
CHATTERBOX	PRESS BOX
GLOVE BOX	SAFE-DEPOSIT BOX
JACK-IN-THE-BOX	SANDBOX
JUKEBOX	SHADOW BOX
MAILBOX	SOAPBOX
MATCHBOX	TOOLBOX
MUSIC BOX	VOICE BOX
PANDORA'S BOX	WINDOW BOX
PENALTY BOX	WITNESS-BOX

10. HAPPY BIRTHDAY!

```
N  S  G  E  H  W  S  R  E  P  G
O  D  R  A  T  A  N  I  P  N  T
P  R  P  E  B  O  T  P  I  E  L
F  A  M  I  L  Y  E  S  S  W  P
S  C  R  H  O  H  D  I  A  V  I
O  N  E  T  O  G  R  O  W  O  N
E  A  O  L  Y  P  O  T  O  C  T
R  O  F  I  R  C  B  I  E  G  H
A  R  T  U  T  H  A  L  D  C  E
E  H  S  I  W  A  E  K  A  M  T
Y  A  G  Y  H  B  R  N  E  S  A
E  L  I  I  R  O  D  O  V  E  I
N  L  F  A  O  L  R  N  C  G  L
O  N  T  H  E  D  O  N  K  E  Y
E  E  S  S  K  N  A  P  S  R  D
```

CAKE	MAKE A WISH
CANDLES	ON THE DONKEY
CARDS	ONE TO GROW ON
CELEBRATE	ONE YEAR
DECORATIONS	PARTY
FAMILY	PIN THE TAIL
GIFTS	PIÑATA
GOODY BAG	SING
HATS	SPANKS
HORNS	SURPRISE

11. IN THE GARDEN

```
C  Q  S  U  G  O  T  E  F  R  O
O  M  A  B  S  N  U  T  R  S  P
M  T  R  E  L  L  I  S  E  H  L
P  F  E  O  N  U  R  L  H  R  A
O  D  E  I  I  C  B  H  P  H  N
S  A  R  R  A  A  D  D  O  A  T
T  R  O  O  T  S  I  S  G  R  S
A  N  E  E  N  I  E  I  H  P  G
S  A  G  W  U  V  L  E  R  A  U
R  E  O  S  O  C  K  I  G  A  L
V  K  V  H  F  L  N  R  Z  D  S
E  A  N  O  L  K  F  A  S  E  T
W  R  E  V  L  E  K  T  N  H  R
R  E  E  E  O  G  L  I  O  S  F
T  H  R  L  E  M  V  D  I  E  D
```

BULBS	ROOTS
COMPOST	SAPLING
FERTILIZER	SEEDS
FLOWERS	SHOVEL
FOUNTAIN	SLUGS
GLOVES	SOIL
GOPHER	SPRINKLER
HOSE	TRELLIS
PLANTS	VEGETABLES
RAKE	VINES

12. WEDDING BELLS

```
T  H  E  N  O  I  L  B  Y  D
T  H  N  E  B  O  U  Q  U  E  T
P  O  W  W  E  O  R  V  I  K  E
M  S  S  T  O  R  E  R  D  A  I
N  A  R  D  Y  G  R  E  L  C  M
G  N  I  C  N  A  D  H  E  B  Y
T  H  N  D  M  E  I  P  F  S  S
S  T  G  T  O  A  I  A  T  E  I
N  T  S  O  W  F  M  R  P  R  B
O  U  N  N  E  I  H  G  F  E  O
J  X  U  E  L  N  E  O  S  C  E
Y  E  O  Y  S  D  U  T  N  V  H
U  D  S  B  I  E  M  O  A  O  N
D  O  A  R  A  A  R  H  N  W  R
D  W  B  A  N  D  I  P  F  S  E
```

AISLE	GOWN
BAND	GROOM
BEST MAN	JUST MARRIED
BOUQUET	LIMO
BRIDE	MAID OF HONOR
CAKE	PHOTOGRAPHER
CLERGY	PRESENTS
DANCING	RINGS
FAMILY	TUXEDO
FRIENDS	VOWS

13. SCHOOL DAZE

```
L  B  L  U  N  C  H  L  Y  I  H
A  L  V  E  H  T  A  M  L  E  N
E  A  E  A  N  V  E  A  B  E  R
L  C  L  T  E  G  P  T  M  M  B
Y  K  S  K  D  I  L  C  E  H  G
O  B  O  O  C  N  L  I  S  I  Y
N  O  G  N  V  I  A  N  S  T  M
B  A  I  S  A  E  R  W  A  H  C
F  R  E  H  C  A  E  T  O  E  L
P  D  R  E  A  I  W  M  I  H  A
T  N  O  I  T  N  E  T  E  D  S
H  M  Y  T  I  W  E  N  D  K  S
U  R  E  P  O  R  T  C  C  S  A
T  S  I  R  N  G  R  A  D  E  S
T  O  K  N  M  T  W  A  I  D  N
```

ASSEMBLY	HOMEWORK
BELL	LUNCH
BLACKBOARD	MATH
BOOK	PRINCIPAL
CHALK	REPORT
DESK	SCIENCE
DETENTION	SHOW-AND-TELL
ENGLISH	TEACHER
GRADES	TEST
GYM CLASS	VACATION

14. GUESS THE THEME 1

For instructions on how to solve Guess the Theme puzzles, see page 6. The word list is on page 63.

```
T  T  N  A  L  P  G  G  E  H  E
W  O  L  A  L  C  O  F  F  E  E
R  N  O  E  A  D  L  I  S  T  R
T  C  E  V  B  C  O  K  N  E  T
A  A  I  V  R  E  I  N  D  T  N
S  A  H  T  A  H  T  I  S  W  C
R  Y  I  P  D  R  P  A  N  O  H
E  G  K  S  O  S  O  I  R  D  A
P  T  H  S  R  T  A  D  O  A  L
P  A  T  A  T  R  E  N  A  H  K
E  L  N  N  L  H  Y  I  O  S  B
P  R  R  T  M  X  G  O  S  T  O
N  U  N  S  H  A  B  I  T  L  A
B  Y  B  L  A  E  B  O  N  Y  R
L  I  O  E  D  U  R  C  C  K  D
```

B____ _____   L_____
   C_____   N____ ___
C_____   N__'_ _____
     C___   O___
   C_____   P_____
C____ ___   P_____
     E____   R____
   E_____   S_____
   I____ ___   S_____
K_____ ____   T__ ___

15. MONKEY BUSINESS

```
G  W  P  E  E  H  C  E  E  H  C
H  N  A  R  S  C  O  P  E  S  U
S  G  O  R  I  L  L  A  T  C  R
E  E  K  K  I  M  R  N  A  H  I
P  D  E  O  Y  N  A  N  F  I  O
A  M  O  N  O  E  A  T  N  M  U
L  I  V  E  O  N  K  A  E  P  S
N  L  V  K  A  E  T  N  E  Y  G
I  I  I  B  S  U  V  A  O  J  E
L  N  B  R  G  L  E  I  U  D  O
T  A  O  N  D  F  L  N  L  B  R
Y  Z  A  K  I  N  G  K  O  N  G
A  R  H  O  T  L  A  N  O  A  E
O  A  I  R  E  B  O  M  A  K  B
O  T  N  O  B  B  I  G  O  N  O
```

APES	JUNGLE
BANANA	KING KONG
BONOBO	KOKO
CHEE-CHEE	MANDRILL
CHIMP	ORANGUTAN
CURIOUS GEORGE	PRIMATE
DONKEY KONG	SCOPES
GIBBON	SEE NO EVIL
GORILLA	SPEAK NO EVIL
HEAR NO EVIL	TARZAN

16. ZZZZZZZZZZZZ

```
I  D  R  W  E  M  A  M  M  E  D
I  T  A  P  A  J  A  M  A  S  T
Y  A  H  E  H  T  T  I  H  E  A
D  T  R  G  T  H  E  U  G  F  E
R  D  E  R  I  M  M  R  O  A  R
O  S  E  D  I  L  H  R  B  M  T
W  S  A  T  D  L  T  I  R  E  D
S  G  D  G  L  Y  Y  H  K  O  D
Y  E  N  N  W  W  B  N  G  W  H
B  E  N  I  I  O  A  E  W  I  O
K  Y  N  S  N  L  L  E  A  U  N
P  K  R  S  B  R  L  L  M  R  W
S  Y  P  O  K  N  U  B  I  I  A
L  L  O  T  T  W  L  T  W  P  Y
A  E  R  O  N  S  S  G  O  N  E
```

BEDTIME	PAJAMAS
BLANKET	PILLOW
BUNK	SNORE
DREAM	STORY
DROWSY	TEDDY BEAR
FORTY WINKS	TIRED
HIT THE HAY	TOSSING
LULLABY	TURNING
MATTRESS	WATERBED
NIGHT-LIGHT	YAWN

17. FINGER FUN

```
M  A  B  U  R  N  C  H  O  F  E
B  A  A  I  N  A  N  K  A  C  T
S  I  N  T  S  K  N  R  A  N  N
O  G  W  I  N  U  X  E  D  N  I
A  S  Y  C  C  A  P  M  H  N  O
A  N  D  K  A  U  N  O  O  D  P
I  K  L  L  N  N  R  T  D  I  I
I  E  E  E  V  I  T  E  N  I  A
O  K  A  Y  D  U  P  C  S  U  N
A  L  B  A  B  N  H  O  S  O  O
B  A  N  H  H  O  A  N  S  A  L
R  M  S  S  C  R  A  T  C  H  E
C  U  U  A  U  P  L  R  L  E  D
P  F  I  H  O  N  G  O  D  E  R
S  G  N  I  T  I  B  L  I  A  N
```

INDEX	PINKY
KEYBOARD	POINT
KNUCKLE	PUSH-BUTTON
"LOSER"	REMOTE CONTROL
MANICURE	RING
NAIL-BITING	SCRATCH
"OKAY"	SNAP
"PEACE"	THUMB
PIANO	TICKLE
PINCH	TOUCH

18. SMALL POTATOES

```
I  T  K  T  R  I  F  L  I  N  G
M  S  A  N  S  M  A  A  I  L  L
W  I  O  R  I  I  L  T  D  B  D
U  T  N  I  V  D  S  W  O  I  U
M  B  L  I  D  Y  Y  N  N  T  W
E  I  R  A  B  N  T  K  Y  T  M
A  T  N  I  O  P  Y  S  N  C  I
S  E  T  O  A  I  N  N  T  I  C
L  S  I  L  R  E  I  T  C  M  R
Y  I  E  I  E  L  T  O  I  O  O
R  Z  M  T  Y  E  E  N  D  T  I
T  E  A  T  I  N  U  A  S  A  T
L  D  T  L  E  T  V  E  G  B  N
A  E  P  E  E  W  E  E  W  U  R
P  I  G  H  Y  N  U  P  T  S  E
```

BITE-SIZED	PEEWEE
DINKY	PETITE
ITSY-BITSY	PETTY
LITTLE	PUNY
MEASLY	RINKY-DINK
MICRO	SUBATOMIC
MINI	TEENSY
MINOR-LEAGUE	TINY
MINUTE	TRIFLING
PALTRY	TRIVIAL

24

19. "HOW ARE YOU FEELING?"

```
S  L  A  S  D  T  J  N  I  G  H
D  I  T  B  D  E  T  I  C  X  E
E  D  L  A  A  T  T  W  B  E
R  L  E  L  V  S  E  O  I  L  F
A  E  O  V  Y  L  H  T  V  U  I
C  U  M  M  E  E  N  F  S  E  E
S  U  O  I  C  I  P  S  U  S  D
B  T  F  U  T  P  L  N  D  L  Y
G  R  U  M  P  Y  R  E  O  W  P
I  F  N  B  E  D  S  A  R  E  P
L  L  N  I  B  U  K  B  H  E  A
T  M  Y  H  F  O  O  L  I  S  H
I  L  R  N  T  R  R  Y  C  E  N
T  A  O  S  E  P  G  N  E  O  R
G  C  E  D  R  I  E  W  A  D  E
```

BASHFUL	HAPPY
BLUE	JEALOUS
BORED	PROUD
CALM	RELIEVED
CONFUSED	SCARED
DEVOTED	SHARP
EXCITED	SILLY
FOOLISH	STUBBORN
FUNNY	SUSPICIOUS
GRUMPY	WEIRD

20. GET A CLUE

Just like the classic boardgame, you've got to answer the question posed in the word list.

```
P  L  U  M  C  A  U  T  L  G  H
T  E  N  E  H  C  T  I  K  C  O
L  A  O  M  N  E  B  N  L  M  U
Y  D  D  O  B  R  M  U  S  M  T
A  P  R  O  A  D  D  D  O  I  D
I  I  T  R  E  V  L  O  V  E  R
I  P  Y  D  N  E  R  H  T  H  M
N  E  E  R  G  G  E  W  C  O  O
N  T  S  A  N  N  E  R  O  P  E
S  R  E  I  C  U  E  R  K  V  A
T  T  N  L  O  O  L  T  N  R  Y
U  I  W  L  R  L  C  I  I  T  H
D  T  L  I  A  A  H  K  F  H  E
Y  A  C  B  A  H  C  N  E  R  W
H  N  D  L  E  S  T  S  I  C  K
```

BALL ROOM	MR. BODDY
BILLIARD ROOM	PEACOCK
DINING ROOM	PLUM
GREEN	REVOLVER
HALL	ROPE
KITCHEN	SCARLET
KNIFE	STUDY
LEAD PIPE	WHITE
LIBRARY	WHODUNIT?
LOUNGE	WRENCH

21. BRITISH-AMERICAN QUIZ

Can you match the American words with their British slang counterparts? Solve the puzzle to find the answers.

```
T  A  L  F  T  S  L  O  R  R  Y
H  R  E  A  P  N  O  S  W  E  R
S  A  U  I  H  C  R  O  T  R  E
O  N  H  C  E  R  T  N  C  Y  T
S  C  O  O  K  I  E  W  P  O  A
T  E  L  H  R  M  P  P  G  E  B
E  L  I  F  T  G  A  F  A  I  O
R  U  D  R  R  N  W  E  S  I  F
O  I  A  E  F  R  V  C  O  E  D
T  P  Y  N  E  H  U  J  L  S  I
A  X  B  N  S  I  C  E  I  V  E
V  A  C  A  T  I  O  N  N  N  H
E  H  E  P  I  G  H  T  E  F  N
L  I  N  S  E  D  T  E  N  R  I
E  T  H  G  I  L  H  S  A  L  F
```

1. APARTMENT	a. BISCUIT
2. COOKIE	b. CHIPS
3. DIAPER	c. FLAT
4. ELEVATOR	d. HOLIDAY
5. FLASHLIGHT	e. LIFT
6. FRENCH FRIES	f. LORRY
7. GASOLINE	g. NAPPY
8. TRUCK	h. PETROL
9. VACATION	i. SPANNER
10. WRENCH	j. TORCH

22. HORSEY SET

```
A  H  O  R  S  D  E  R  M  E  A
L  S  H  S  O  N  R  S  E  G  M
C  E  N  T  A  U  R  S  I  Y  Y
K  V  S  M  I  D  N  D  S  G  T
H  O  I  U  D  O  D  P  M  R  U
O  O  L  F  O  Y  U  L  O  O  A
B  H  V  R  U  R  A  J  E  H  E
B  T  E  P  R  E  A  O  R  S  B
Y  E  R  I  R  N  L  C  F  I  K
H  W  T  I  H  C  S  D  L  H  C
O  S  H  O  G  A  N  R  I  S  A
R  D  R  O  I  G  I  I  C  R  L
S  S  U  S  A  G  E  P  K  U  B
E  I  A  C  T  V  R  R  A  P  S
C  E  N  E  I  T  U  O  C  S  V
```

BLACK BEAUTY	PEGASUS
BRIDLE	REINS
CAROUSEL	SADDLE
CENTAURS	SCOUT
FLICKA	SILVER
"GIDDYUP!"	SPURS
HOBBYHORSE	STIRRUPS
HOOVES	TRIGGER
MANE	TROJAN HORSE
MR. ED	"WHOA!"

23. LET'S EAT OUT TONIGHT

```
S  P  E  C  I  A  L  S  D  K  I
N  E  R  L  N  R  W  K  C  U  Y
H  A  E  E  L  A  T  I  T  I  S
T  H  T  A  I  I  P  S  H  F  L
D  R  I  N  K  H  B  K  G  Y  D
A  O  A  Y  T  I  O  S  I  E  S
P  N  W  O  G  I  O  N  A  N  A
P  M  O  U  Y  U  S  S  R  T  L
E  T  O  R  P  U  T  M  T  R  A
T  L  P  P  T  R  E  S  S  E  D
I  W  B  L  A  N  R  I  P  E  T
Z  C  E  A  U  R  S  T  U  H  T
E  E  H  T  T  B  E  A  T  N  C
R  E  S  E  R  V  A  T  I  O  N
K  S  T  R  F  O  T  M  S  K  E
```

APPETIZER	NAPKIN
BILL	RESERVATION
BOOSTER SEAT	SALAD
CHEF	"SIT UP STRAIGHT"
"CLEAN YOUR PLATE"	SOUP
DESSERT	SPECIALS
DRINK	TABLE
ENTRÉE	TOOTHPICK
MENU	WAITER
MINT	"YUCK!"

24. SPORTS EQUIPMENT

```
N  I  T  H  K  E  S  W  S  W  O
P  O  S  E  H  O  I  L  O  G  O
W  O  K  L  K  C  A  A  D  S  S
D  I  L  M  K  C  E  R  S  I  K
B  G  R  E  M  M  A  H  S  B  A
N  E  T  T  V  O  D  R  A  B  T
H  Y  C  A  B  O  R  L  O  L  E
Y  U  N  F  D  A  L  V  I  D  S
S  O  R  N  W  H  O  G  W  A  R
A  U  S  D  P  A  I  P  D  T  E
S  T  A  E  L  C  H  A  I  R  P
B  T  S  Y  F  E  L  D  D  A  P
U  I  V  E  E  D  S  S  O  U  I
L  D  I  S  C  U  S  L  C  L  L
C  A  R  S  F  O  R  K  I  T  F
```

BALL	HURDLES
BIKE	OARS
CESTA	PADDLE
CLEATS	PADS
CLUBS	POLE
DISCUS	PUCK
FLIPPERS	RACKET
GLOVE	SKATES
HAMMER	SURFBOARD
HELMET	WICKET

25. INANIMATE SPORTS TEAMS

```
A  B  O  U  T  B  F  T  O  M  R
T  Y  F  S  P  U  R  S  A  I  V
S  E  P  S  E  L  R  P  C  E  E
N  T  T  A  R  L  L  O  F  A  H
M  E  A  B  S  E  M  A  L  F  R
A  I  S  R  L  T  P  C  A  N  S
S  V  O  E  S  S  S  P  W  N  T
P  A  A  S  I  T  N  I  I  X  E
I  F  T  L  E  K  E  M  O  L  K
S  W  I  G  A  T  C  S  H  A  C
T  T  G  T  C  N  E  O  J  E  O
O  U  E  I  S  T  C  E  R  A  R
N  M  G  N  I  N  T  H  G  I  L
S  A  L  H  O  S  U  G  E  O  O
M  N  W  I  R  E  D  S  O  X  T
```

AVALANCHE	NUGGETS
BULLETS	PISTONS
CLIPPERS	RED SOX
FLAMES	ROCKETS
HEAT	ROCKIES
JETS	SABRES
LIGHTNING	SPURS
MAGIC	STARS
MAPLE LEAFS	SUNS
NETS	WHITE SOX

26. SLOW DOWN!

```
S  W  H  A  G  L  A  C  I  E  R
E  E  T  A  N  A  M  T  K  D  O
E  S  S  Z  A  M  B  O  N  I  A
Y  S  S  S  N  A  P  H  N  I  E
L  E  S  A  A  W  S  C  Y  G  W
H  K  L  E  O  L  H  R  R  E  S
N  A  I  L  O  W  O  A  T  L  P
R  R  S  T  O  I  B  M  U  D  A
L  B  H  R  E  W  S  G  O  N  R
A  I  M  U  A  T  L  N  U  R  A
I  T  A  T  I  H  C  I  A  T  C
D  O  W  N  L  O  A  D  G  L  H
N  E  S  B  S  A  C  D  K  H  U
U  W  P  A  R  A  D  E  H  E  T
S  N  O  W  P  L  O  W  E  E  E
```

BARGE	SLOWPOKE
BRAKES	SLUG
DOWNLOAD	SNAIL
GLACIER	SNOWPLOW
INCHWORM	SUNDIAL
MANATEE	TAI CHI
MOLASSES	TURTLE
PARACHUTE	WEDDING MARCH
PARADE	YELLOW LIGHT
SLOTH	ZAMBONI

27. VALENTINE'S DAY

```
        C A M       O O R
      V I A N C   T E E W S
    S E M Y R R A M I A T O M
  N G S V I A D O I S C N L A T
  I U W N O F R H O R A L G O V
  C H O C O L A T E E N I M E B
  Y E R C O S D N A H D L O H L
    R R K I S S E S N Y Q U C
      A E D S R E W O L F R
        U R I S T B E A U
          R A P R L L S
            B L U S H
              E O C
                F
```

ANGEL	FEBRUARY
ARROWS	FLOWERS
BEAU	FOURTEENTH
"BE MINE"	HOLD HANDS
BLUSH	HUGS
CANDY	KISSES
CARD	LOVE
CHOCOLATE	"MARRY ME"
CRUSH	ROMEO
CUPID	SWEET

28. THE PLAY'S THE THING

```
A  C  C  I  S  U  M  T  I  N  P
G  L  I  G  H  T  S  A  D  R  R
E  V  I  C  E  I  L  H  A  E  O
C  M  A  W  N  R  S  T  E  S  P
N  N  U  G  O  Y  S  G  O  R  S
A  U  R  T  I  B  A  L  O  I  G
D  N  Y  E  S  T  A  G  S  E  A
A  N  A  D  S  O  R  E  L  D  C
C  U  W  O  I  A  C  A  K  N  U
T  T  D  B  M  U  K  M  P  A  R
O  I  A  I  R  A  N  T  O  T  T
R  H  O  E  E  F  K  U  R  N  A
I  T  R  R  T  N  U  E  R  E  I
N  O  B  E  N  L  C  C  U  O  N
W  A  R  T  I  C  K  E  T  P  D
```

ACTOR	MUSIC
AUDIENCE	PROGRAM
"BREAK A LEG"	PROPS
BROADWAY	SETS
COSTUME	SING
CURTAIN	STAGE
DANCE	STAR
INTERMISSION	"TAKE A BOW"
LIGHTS	TICKET
MAKEUP	USHER

29. JUST PLAIN MEAN

```
J  F  K  D  Q  U  M  M  O  T  N
S  P  I  K  E  J  O  E  F  O  A
B  R  G  S  C  R  O  O  G  E  H
S  I  I  V  I  E  D  K  Y  O  K
C  U  G  A  I  R  R  R  E  O  E
A  R  R  B  E  H  D  N  O  R  R
R  T  U  E  A  M  S  H  I  M  E
Y  L  E  E  R  D  N  I  S  B  H
U  T  U  A  L  I  W  N  K  E  S
V  D  F  T  A  L  E  O  A  I  N
D  A  R  T  H  M  A  U  L  R  R
J  F  P  E  O  R  G  U  F  U
E  A  T  T  V  H  R  E  S  I  B
C  R  H  C  N  I  R  G  N  R
A  M  E  S  G  O  L  L  U  M  M
```

BIG BAD WOLF	LUTHOR
CAPTAIN HOOK	MORDRED
CRUELLA	MORIARTY
DARTH MAUL	MR. BURNS
DR. DOOM	RIKISHI
DR. EVIL	SCAR
GOLLUM	SCROOGE
GRINCH	SHERE KHAN
JAFAR	SPIKE
JOKER	URSULA

30. GUESS THE THEME 2

For instructions on how to solve Guess the Theme puzzles, see page 6. The word list is on page 63.

```
T  D  R  A  C  T  S  O  P  H  E
W  O  R  I  G  A  M  I  W  O  P
R  A  D  A  L  I  S  T  C  O  M
N  T  S  A  O  W  I  S  N  K  A
L  N  P  P  A  B  E  S  I  I  T
U  T  I  R  N  H  D  T  K  E  S
N  M  T  S  C  E  E  R  P  T  C
C  S  B  T  T  R  S  H  A  A  O
H  A  A  T  E  K  A  T  N  C  N
B  M  L  T  M  O  I  R  E  O  F
A  R  L  E  P  O  L  E  V  N  E
G  I  C  A  N  B  N  E  N  B  T
F  E  M  E  A  D  D  E  B  E  T
O  F  R  P  A  P  A  E  Y  A  I
R  Y  E  N  A  L  P  R  I  A  L
```

A _ _ _ _ _ _ _   M _ _ _ _ _ _
  B _ _ _   M _ _ _ _
C _ _ _ _ _ _ _   N _ _ _ _ _
C _ _ _ _ _ _ _ _   O _ _ _ _ _ _
C _ _ _ _ _ _ _   P _ _ _ _ _ _ _
E _ _ _ _ _ _ _   S _ _ _ _ _ _ _
  F _ _ _ _ _   S _ _ _ _
   K _ _ _   S _ _ _ _ _ _ _ _ _
   L _ _ _ _   S _ _ _ _
L _ _ _ _ _ _ _   W _ _ _ _ _ _ _

31. CROSSWORDSEARCH

In this puzzle, the words in the grid are clued as in a crossword puzzle. (Hint: The answers are in alphabetical order.) The word list is on page 64.

```
            C  R  U  L  C
            I  Q  O  V  E
            R  S  U  T  N
            S  P  B  I  A
            E  H  C  B  T
M  L  I  S  R  V  K  S  B  H  C  N  E  R  F
T  O  C  S  G  E  E  N  A  S  E  O  V  M  E
O  N  O  O  L  N  T  E  R  H  W  A  O  H  O
D  N  E  Z  N  Y  M  T  C  E  U  S  D  I  G
N  S  C  R  O  S  A  T  U  L  A  M  M  A  M
            S  I  R  T  B
            K  L  D  X  U
            S  L  N  E  O
            W  I  O  R  R
            J  W  D  S  T
```

It's spread on bread   B _ _ _ _ _

Think about   C _ _ _ _ _ _ _

Symbol of peace   D _ _ _

Like fries or toast   F _ _ _ _ _

TV and movie star Davis   G _ _ _ _

Breakfast side dish   H _ _ _

Bad luck charm   J _ _ _

Refrigerator's place   K _ _ _ _ _ _

Failure to win   L _ _ _

The hare, but not the tortoise   M _ _ _ _ _

Thomas Jefferson is on it   N _ _ _ _ _

You, but not the tortoise   P _ _ _ _ _

Give up   Q _ _ _

The hare, but not you   R _ _ _ _ _

Number of dwarfs   S _ _ _ _

Bother   T _ _ _ _ _ _

Strong safe   V _ _ _ _

Shakespeare's first name   W _ _ _ _ _ _

Bone picture   X - _ _ _

TV show for kids   Z _ _ _

32. GET YOUR PAPER HERE!

```
A  L  L  T  W  H  E  N  E  R  C
W  S  T  E  G  A  P  D  E  P  O
H  S  A  X  D  T  N  P  S  F  L
I  O  T  T  T  I  O  T  O  P  U
R  T  I  R  S  R  T  N  A  T  M
D  O  R  A  T  T  I  O  B  D  N
E  H  S  E  T  H  R  Y  R  E  S
A  P  R  S  V  P  L  O  L  O  C
R  S  O  G  A  I  W  N  P  O  I
A  F  T  C  N  S  E  H  E  S  M
B  Y  N  E  S  S  E  W  W  L  O
B  Y  L  O  P  O  O  C  S  O  C
Y  O  R  I  R  G  R  K  T  C  I
M  C  E  N  A  T  I  O  N  A  L
S  E  N  I  L  D  A  E  H  L  S
```

BYLINE	HOROSCOPE
COLUMNS	LOCAL
COMICS	NATIONAL
CROSSWORD	OP-ED PAGE
DAILY	PHOTOS
"DEAR ABBY"	REPORTERS
EDITOR	REVIEWS
EXTRA	SCOOP
GOSSIP	SPORTS
HEADLINES	WANT ADS

33. ART CLASS

```
M T H L E F O U R T E
E O S K E T C H Y N A
G E D M U S T P R A O
N S L E T S A P E I T
N F C N L L I E L N J
W R I I E A T S L U R
T A L T L E S A A R E
P M T N N Y C I G A B
M E E E D F R O R F R
A M N P R B A C O S U
U I M R R C Y S A P S
L S T U D I O V A I H
N T S T R E N L R S E
A H N D S A K C O M S
C U L P C T L O R R S
```

ACRYLICS	MURAL
AIRBRUSH	OILS
BRUSHES	PAINT
CANVAS	PALETTE
CRAYON	PASTEL
EASEL	SKETCH
FRAME	SMOCK
GALLERY	STUDIO
LINE	TURPENTINE
MODEL	WATERCOLOR

34. SNOW TIME

```
I  S  N  S  T  Y  H  E  S  O  N
G  D  L  F  L  R  R  O  S  B  T
Y  T  R  E  Z  E  E  R  F  A  H
E  S  N  A  D  O  V  W  U  L  M
A  N  H  W  Z  A  S  O  A  L  A
M  R  O  T  S  Z  C  O  H  V  F
R  P  N  U  L  C  I  O  A  S  L
B  P  I  O  P  L  B  L  E  A  A
N  D  T  E  K  N  A  L  B  A  K
B  U  T  T  T  N  N  U  O  N  E
S  N  O  I  C  S  K  E  Q  A  H
N  L  D  H  T  F  I  R  D  S  T
W  O  E  W  E  Y  A  E  U  S  M
A  D  E  E  H  A  I  L  O  U  T
O  F  C  O  T  A  S  A  L  T  L
```

AVALANCHE	HAIL
BALL	POWDER
BANK	SALT
BLANKET	SHOVELS
BLIZZARD	SLED
DRIFT	SLEET
FALL	SLUSH
FLAKE	SQUALL
FLURRY	STORM
FREEZE	WHITEOUT

35. GREETINGS FROM FLORIDA

```
E  R  I  T  E  R  G  T  H  T  E
S  E  N  I  H  S  N  U  S  T  D
A  T  S  E  M  S  O  E  L  L  N
G  K  O  S  F  A  W  F  R  F  T
T  A  M  P  A  Y  I  O  L  A  O
R  E  I  D  E  H  W  M  N  A  I
S  R  S  K  V  Y  A  N  S  T  E
P  B  H  U  E  E  I  L  S  O  N
F  G  O  N  R  N  S  R  L  R  J
T  N  S  E  G  F  O  R  S  A  O
L  I  D  W  L  T  F  E  G  N  T
D  R  B  E  A  C  H  U  L  G  O
A  P  L  G  D  M  A  K  S  E  A
H  S  T  H  E  R  P  O  M  S  D
C  A  L  U  S  N  I  N  E  P  E
```

BEACH	ORANGES
CHAD	PENINSULA
DE LEÓN	RETIRE
DISNEY WORLD	SPRING BREAK
EVERGLADES	SUNSHINE
GATORS	SURF
GULF	SWAMP
JAGUARS	TALLAHASSEE
KEY WEST	TAMPA
MIAMI	TANNING

36. GOING BATTY

Each entry in the list contains the word BAT, but in the grid, every BAT appears as a 🦇 symbol. For example, if BATTER were in the list, it would appear in the grid as 🦇TER.

```
V  A  E  M  P  I  R  M  E  C  C
S  U  N 🦇  H  E  E  P  H  I  I
L  D  R  E  U  L  N  R  L  M  E
H  A  C  R 🦇  C  N  O  T  O  H
A  E  A  O  L  P  N 🦇  H 🦇  A
V 🦇  A  I  M  N  S  I  E  U  P
Z  S  T  A  L 🦇  R  O  S  S 🦇
T  E  D  W  M  S  B  N  T  B  M
I  E  O  E  A  E 🦇  O  R  C  A
M  M  R  B 🦇  R  B  T  O  H  N
🦇  E 🦇  T  Y  E  W  O  E  T  A
R  H  A  G  L 🦇  T  E  R  Y  S
🦇  P  T  T  N  E  O  E  S  H  C
U  H 🦇  D  R  I  B  H  A  O 🦇
O  L  C  L  O  T  D  H  E  M  S
```

ACROBAT	DINGBAT
ALBATROSS	INCUBATE
BATHROBE	MELBA TOAST
BATMAN	PROBATION
BAT MITZVAH	REBATE
BATTERY	SABBATH
BATTLEBOTS	SUBATOMIC
BIRDBATH	SUNBATHE
COMBAT BOOTS	UP AT BAT
DEBATE TEAM	WOMBAT

37. TRIOS

```
T  H  R  E  K  B  E  A  R  S  E
T  H  I  I  N  T  G  S  G  R  S
I  S  N  O  S  S  E  I  C  E  A
N  G  N  E  E  R  P  N  K  V  V
S  N  E  R  M  E  R  I  O  I  E
F  I  D  D  L  E  R  S  S  R  C
B  R  M  T  S  T  S  Y  E  H  S
M  L  T  B  S  E  E  I  I  E  R
N  I  I  A  M  K  G  P  W  E  S
L  S  F  N  N  S  M  O  A  F  R
C  E  S  O  D  U  P  A  O  A  E
N  D  M  I  N  M  F  I  O  T  T
R  G  O  K  T  W  I  S  H  E  S
T  H  S  E  T  H  I  C  R  S  I
D  B  U  T  A  N  I  N  E  M  S
```

BEARS	RINGS
BLIND MICE	RIVERS
CHIPMUNKS	SHIPS
FATES	SISTERS
FIDDLERS	SONS
KINGS	STOOGES
LITTLE PIGS	STRIKES
MEN IN A TUB	TENORS
MONKEYS	WISE MEN
MUSKETEERS	WISHES

38. GUESS THE THEME 3

For instructions on how to solve Guess the Theme puzzles, see page 6. The word list is on page 63.

```
G  T  C  H  A  I  S  E  H  I  S
N  G  B  R  A  T  I  N  D  C  E
I  R  O  E  O  M  N  A  T  S  A
W  I  E  I  N  N  M  M  R  R  S
S  E  L  C  Y  C  R  O  T  O  M
E  E  P  A  L  A  H  T  C  C  L
T  L  A  H  F  I  S  T  L  K  O
T  R  L  O  C  T  N  O  S  E  O
E  F  S  T  C  R  V  E  L  R  T
E  H  A  I  U  E  U  C  R  N  G
S  L  T  T  S  F  Y  H  H  A  T
P  O  N  E  H  C  F  E  C  O  P
L  O  A  E  I  C  O  E  M  M  O
N  T  S  B  O  L  Y  S  T  I  T
U  S  P  E  N  O  R  H  T  O  N
```

B _ _ _ _   R _ _ _ _ _ _
B _ _ _ _ _ _   R _ _ _ _ _
C _ _ _ _ _   S _ _ _ _ ' _ _ _ _
C _ _ _ _ _ _ _ _   S _ _ _ _ _ _
C _ _ _ _ _ _   S _ _ _
H _ _ _ _ _ _   S _ _ _ _
  H _ _ _ _   S _ _ _ _
L _ _ _ _ _ _ _   T _ _ _ _ _
M _ _ _ _ _ _ _ _ _   T _ _ _ _ _
  O _ _ _ _ _ _   T _ _ _ _ _

44

39. AW, NUTS!

```
    N  A  P  I  Z  R  A  M  C
 M  A  R  R  O  N  O  C  O  D  E
 M  C  N  O  U  G  A  T  I  E  R
 A  E  P  V  C  E  R  H  F  A  Y
 T  P  I  S  T  A  C  H  I  O  R
    U  G  A  L  T  S  M  L  R
       N  M  I  E  A  H  B
       O  L  Z  D  C  O  E
    N  L  C  A  O  N  C  R  W
 D  U  I  C  R  W  T  O  T  V  A
 R  I  A  E  B  T  Y  C  K  I  S
 T  M  S  R  E  B  O  O  G  H  E
 W  O  R  L  T  D  L  N  S  L  A
 R  G  E  P  E  A  N  U  T  S  T
    S  H  E  L  L  N  T  U  T
```

ACORN	MACADAMIA
ALMOND	MARRON
BETEL	MARZIPAN
BRAZIL	NOUGAT
CASHEW	PEANUT
COCONUT	PECAN
FILBERT	PIGNOLIA
GOOBERS	PISTACHIO
KOLA	SHELL
LITCHI	WALNUT

40. EEEK!

```
W  N  H  E  K  T  F  N  P  F  T
E  H  E  E  E  L  R  E  B  L  E
E  S  R  E  E  L  E  C  T  E  T
C  G  P  E  T  D  E  E  T  E  T
M  E  R  E  E  N  V  N  N  C  S
E  T  E  E  S  S  E  N  N  E  T
E  D  N  T  P  E  R  V  H  W  X
W  K  E  Y  W  E  S  N  E  E  R
N  E  D  T  V  E  E  E  R  S  E
E  C  E  E  R  G  D  K  R  S  P
E  B  C  K  E  L  S  T  E  T  E
T  H  R  E  E  K  E  E  E  E  E
E  E  E  D  N  N  H  V  E  S  B
R  T  E  P  E  C  D  R  E  S  E
P  E  E  W  E  E  V  E  R  E  E
```

BEEKEEPER	KNEE-DEEP
BEEPER	LEVEE
BETWEEN	PEEWEE
CHEESE	PRETEEN
DECREE	REELECT
EMCEE	SEVENTEEN
FLEECE	TEEPEE
FREE VERSE	TENNESSEE
GREECE	TWEEDLEDEE
KLEENEX	WEEKEND

41. SIX-LETTER WORLD CAPITALS

```
M  A  O  R  E  M  W  O  R  L  D
C  N  A  Z  A  G  R  E  B  P  I
T  N  A  D  L  N  A  M  E  S  B
E  E  R  G  D  M  I  N  W  L  I
T  I  A  W  U  K  O  T  I  O  H
D  V  R  T  B  A  H  S  E  N  A
L  E  A  T  L  T  B  H  C  D  E
R  S  K  I  I  O  B  D  N  O  T
H  A  N  N  N  A  N  A  Y  N  W
O  A  A  E  O  I  U  Y  T  A  H
M  T  E  U  H  L  L  I  S  R  L
I  K  T  G  E  T  U  R  I  E  B
P  A  N  A  M  A  A  B  E  E  R
L  I  N  R  W  W  A  N  D  B  B
E  I  E  P  I  A  T  I  R  U  T
```

ANKARA	MANILA
ATHENS	MOSCOW
BEIRUT	OTTAWA
BERLIN	PANAMA
DUBLIN	PRAGUE
KUWAIT	RIYADH
LISBON	TAIPEI
LONDON	VIENNA
LUANDA	WARSAW
MADRID	ZAGREB

42. WAY TO GO!

```
B  O  F  R  E  P  U  S  B  G  B
F  Y  M  I  C  F  L  E  S  R  W
R  R  Y  L  R  A  N  G  R  O  I
E  N  S  D  M  S  O  N  E  O  B
S  T  T  M  W  H  T  M  K  V  W
H  E  I  O  R  C  S  R  C  Y  I
R  N  Y  M  B  T  E  H  A  A  C
S  O  S  P  A  O  G  P  J  T  K
W  A  T  C  Y  N  W  R  R  O  E
E  N  E  T  E  P  Y  H  E  E  D
E  H  L  D  G  O  R  D  K  A  A
T  M  L  M  Y  T  A  F  C  F  T
O  O  A  R  T  N  P  H  A  T  H
G  E  R  Y  D  E  A  R  R  B  S
B  E  S  Y  T  S  O  N  C  G  U
```

A-ONE	GREAT
BOSS	GROOVY
CRACKERJACK	PHAT
DANDY	SLAMMIN'
DYNAMITE	STELLAR
FABU	SUPER
FIRST-RATE	SWEET
FRESH	THE CAT'S MEOW
GNARLY	TOP-NOTCH
GOLDEN	WICKED

43. WHAT'S THAT ON YOUR HEAD?

```
W  M  Y  T  E  R  E  B  S  E  S
V  I  E  N  N  T  O  U  Y  O  E
I  G  M  H  W  W  T  S  M  Y  E
A  R  O  P  L  O  Y  B  R  E  D
T  L  D  E  L  T  R  Y  G  I  R
U  A  R  O  D  E  F  C  A  P  N
R  D  M  O  R  M  F  A  A  E  T
B  H  O  O  E  L  R  C  B  K  E
A  H  H  A  S  E  T  S  O  I  S
N  R  O  H  M  H  A  N  N  Y  W
D  R  A  I  G  N  A  A  N  K  L
O  K  E  I  S  H  E  N  E  E  H
O  A  N  S  T  B  T  O  T  S  C
N  R  E  K  A  F  F  I  Y  E  H
S  W  H  I  S  H  A  T  O  N  R
```

BEANIE	KAFFIYEH
BERET	KEPI
BONNET	NIGHTCAP
BOWLER	SHAKO
BUSBY	SNOOD
CROWN	SOMBRERO
DERBY	TAM-O'-SHANTER
FEDORA	TIARA
HELMET	TURBAN
HOOD	WIMPLE

44. GUESS THE THEME 4

For instructions on how to solve Guess the Theme puzzles, see page 6. The word list is on page 64.

```
E  T  S  E  P  I  R  T  S  H  H
I  A  P  R  O  U  D  L  Y  A  S
G  R  R  A  A  I  D  G  C  I  G
O  S  N  L  T  M  N  A  I  L  N
S  W  U  G  Y  I  P  O  E  E  R
D  S  F  O  T  R  O  A  E  D  M
T  B  H  S  L  E  M  H  R  U  S
S  N  R  S  A  I  T  O  F  T  I
S  U  O  A  N  O  R  M  R  N  S
B  A  C  G  V  W  L  E  A  N  T
M  T  K  H  E  E  A  M  P  T  A
O  H  E  E  F  M  S  D  T  A  R
B  R  T  W  I  L  I  G  H  T  S
S  P  S  N  D  N  A  L  A  N  G
L  E  G  D  B  A  N  G  N  E  R
```

D _ _ _ ' _   S _ _ _ _ _ _ _ _
E _ _ _ _   R _ _ _ _ _ ' _
P _ _ _ _ _ _   G _ _ _ _
H _ _ _ _ _   B _ _ _ _
T _ _ _ _ _ _ _ ' _   B _ _ _ _ _ _
G _ _ _ _ _ _ _   F _ _ _
S _ _ _ _ _ _   L _ _ _
S _ _ _ _   F _ _ _
P _ _ _ _ _ _ _   H _ _ _
R _ _ _ _ _ _ _   B _ _ _ _

50

45. YIDDISH WORDS

Many of our English words come from French and Latin. Here are a few that come from the Yiddish language.

```
A  P  N  O  K  P  L  T  U  S  H
D  Y  A  C  C  I  E  D  D  I  S
S  H  E  S  I  P  R  L  O  C  A
V  R  H  C  T  I  L  G  H  E  M
D  R  B  H  H  R  M  M  A  C  H
H  A  N  M  S  Y  A  C  L  K  S
O  A  M  O  P  L  L  M  L  A  I
I  N  P  O  T  O  F  U  I  T  M
H  H  Z  Z  E  K  T  I  G  M  A
R  S  T  E  T  Z  O  L  E  O  V
O  K  I  N  D  U  N  S  M  K  E
S  B  B  B  U  T  H  N  H  H  N
O  N  I  E  B  U  O  C  S  E  F
T  H  K  E  G  E  I  O  R  B  R
L  E  G  A  B  R  N  A  I  N  S
```

BAGEL	MISHMASH
CHUTZPAH	NEBBISH
DRECK	NOSH
GLITCH	NUDNIK
KIBITZ	PASTRAMI
KLUTZ	SCHLEP
KOSHER	SCHMALTZ
MAVEN	SCHMOOZE
MEGILLAH	SHTICK
MESHUGA	TUSH

46. JUST DUCKY

```
D  U  C  K  A  S  A  N  D  D  R
A  Y  K  E  S  L  D  H  U  E  Y
K  I  F  S  W  R  U  H  A  I  Y
C  T  S  F  A  K  I  K  M  K  M
U  Q  D  L  A  N  O  D  C  C  D
D  U  L  I  N  D  G  U  S  U  T
C  A  O  E  O  N  L  C  C  D  D
M  C  R  W  I  Y  E  K  A  R  D
E  K  N  K  K  U  D  C  D  E  N
G  E  S  C  W  O  O  A  I  B  O
O  D  U  S  D  I  I  L  I  B  P
O  D  E  G  C  S  N  L  A  U  L
R  L  E  W  Y  E  L  G  D  R  I
C  R  N  E  E  N  G  L  A  N  D
S  K  C  U  D  Y  T  H  G  I  M
```

BILL	DUCKULA
DAFFY	DUCKY LUCKY
DAISY	HUEY
DARKWING	LOUIE
DEWEY	MALLARD
DONALD	MIGHTY DUCKS
DOWN	POND
DRAKE	QUACK
DUCK CALL	RUBBER DUCKIE
DUCK DODGERS	SCROOGE MCDUCK

47. GAS STATION SEARCH

```
T  A  T  E  T  S  N  G  I  S  E
N  F  D  S  N  A  C  K  S  A  N
T  W  I  H  C  A  S  P  A  M  Y
D  T  D  L  O  E  T  S  E  Y  T
G  F  I  L  T  E  R  C  O  O  U
A  O  P  R  R  S  H  A  O  U  L
R  N  S  C  E  A  E  L  R  T  L
A  H  T  A  N  S  S  V  O  L  E
G  E  I  I  U  F  O  W  O  E  B
E  P  C  R  F  I  T  H  G  S  N
T  E  K  D  O  R  N  E  R  E  I
T  A  L  P  U  R  E  L  L  I  F
I  E  N  C  U  U  N  E  L  D  A
E  A  K  D  Q  E  D  F  Z  U  E
L  O  N  S  P  M  U  P  L  E  Y
```

AIRHOSE	MECHANIC
ANTIFREEZE	OCTANE
BELL	OILCAN
DIESEL	PUMPS
DIPSTICK	SIGNS
"FILL 'ER UP"	SNACKS
FILTER	SQUEEGEE
GARAGE	TIRES
LIFT	TOOLS
MAPS	TOW TRUCK

48. BABY ANIMALS

```
R  I  D  D  L  K  K  E  W  E  H
O  I  S  B  I  I  G  R  A  G  E
R  M  C  O  L  T  R  G  I  S  B
I  G  G  T  P  T  L  F  E  T  R
R  E  V  L  E  E  O  I  E  Y  S
R  T  E  C  T  N  M  L  R  P  S
B  H  A  I  H  G  G  L  G  P  D
W  L  E  D  R  I  S  Y  B  U  A
B  Y  A  A  P  N  C  S  C  P  W
E  F  R  M  T  O  H  K  E  B  A
B  O  A  Y  B  B  L  E  C  A  U
F  A  S  W  U  I  E  E  H  E  Y
I  L  S  J  N  U  S  T  A  E  L
I  T  A  G  N  I  L  S  O  G  T
L  E  B  C  Y  I  G  J  G  E  R
```

BUNNY	FOAL
CALF	GOSLING
CHICK	JOEY
COLT	KITTEN
CYGNET	LAMB
DUCKLING	PIGLET
EAGLET	PUPPY
ELVER	STIRK
FAWN	TADPOLE
FILLY	WHELP

49. A NUMBER OF THINGS

```
R  T  E  5  6  3  7  4  2  A  D
D  7  C  T  6  B  H  8  I  9  S
E  6  O  A  U  P  1  U  8  T  L
E  E  O  L  T  K  A  D  U  D  S
P  R  C  O  N  N  E  C  T  4  A
S  S  Q  I  U  G  O  S  K  E  J
0  S  L  T  R  I  I  C  O  N  N
1  B  W  E  7  L  H  Y  1  W  I
A  2  E  S  0  6  R  E  F  2  N
S  S  P  1  0  0  O  A  F  1  3
R  A  P  U  T  I  0  K  D  M  O
7  O  F  9  N  F  7  9  A  A  N
T  P  S  W  E  C  E  C  L  D  R
B  3  5  H  G  I  H  O  E  A  C
A  C  U  S  A  E  7  P  8  9  H
```

ADAM-12	S CLUB 7
AGENT 007	7 OF 9
BLINK 182	76ERS
CONNECT 4	6-PACK
C-3PO	10-SPEED
HAL 9000	3 NINJAS
HIGH 5	3-2-1 CONTACT
K-9 COP	TOP 10 LIST
98 DEGREES	24 7 365
1-2 PUNCH	2-FER

50. LET THERE BE LIGHT

Each entry in the list contains the word LIGHT, but in the grid, every LIGHT appears as a 💡 symbol. For example, if FLASHLIGHT were in the list, it would appear in the grid as FLASH💡.

```
I   F   Y   O   U   G   R   E   N   I   Y
💡  S   O   U   T   N   N   A   E   L   C
M   S   A   💡  Y   K   S   I   💡  R   G
Y   T   P   D   H   B   A   S   N   R   T
F   💡  Y   A   D   L   S   M   E   💡  💡
I   O   V   E   C   U   I   E   N   T   E
R   G   A   H   T   E   N   T   O   H   N
E   S   U   O   H   💡  F   L   E   S   U
P   N   E   E   T   S   I   💡  D   O   P
F   💡  O   H   A   P   D   W   B   R   N
D   Y   G   Z   O   E   U   E   T   A   U
R   I   N   Y   💡  C   O   I   U   E   G
N   R   H   F   E   I   A   G   D   Y   💡
S   O   U   N   W   A   W   H   H   💡  A
T   L   H   A   P   L   P   T   E   N   S
```

BLUE LIGHT SPECIAL	LIGHTNING
DAYLIGHT	"LIGHTS OUT"
DELIGHTFUL	LIGHTWEIGHT
ENLIGHTEN	LIGHT-YEAR
FLIGHT BAG	NIGHT-LIGHT
GREEN LIGHT	PILOT LIGHT
HEADLIGHT	SKYLIGHT
"LIGHTEN UP"	SLIGHTLY
LIGHTHOUSE	SPACEFLIGHT
"LIGHT MY FIRE"	TWILIGHT ZONE

51. SEVEN-LETTER GIRLS' NAMES

```
C  O  R  I  N  N  A  A  R  O  S
A  E  B  N  T  I  F  F  A  N  Y
I  Y  A  N  Y  Y  O  M  T  E  N
T  B  H  E  R  R  N  A  A  T  O
L  M  R  E  W  O  H  R  U  S  S
I  L  E  I  D  S  S  T  M  I  I
N  A  H  G  A  E  M  I  A  R  D
J  E  T  T  L  N  E  N  L  K  A
A  S  A  B  R  I  N  A  A  S  M
C  N  E  S  L  E  W  A  E  A  I
K  E  H  A  R  O  B  E  D  T  R
L  S  T  A  I  D  J  E  U  L  A
Y  A  S  D  N  I  L  I  C  E  N
N  T  T  O  H  Y  E  R  R  C  D
O  M  E  O  N  O  S  I  L  L  A
```

ALLISON	MADELYN
BRIANNA	MADISON
CAITLIN	MARTINA
CORINNA	MEAGHAN
DEBORAH	MIRANDA
HEATHER	NATALIE
JACKLYN	NATASHA
KATHRYN	REBECCA
KRISTEN	SABRINA
LINDSAY	TIFFANY

52. WHAT'S THAT ON THE WALL?

```
G  T  B  H  R  E  K  A  E  P  S
A  U  A  C  I  L  D  I  H  K  H
L  R  E  T  S  O  P  O  C  N  E
F  G  T  I  S  M  T  O  N  T  L
H  E  G  W  R  O  L  A  E  A  F
M  A  P  S  O  C  M  T  W  A  L
L  O  F  C  H  R  I  R  S  N  C
I  A  M  P  E  E  K  C  E  A  O
T  T  A  D  E  T  O  O  L  H  A
O  S  I  G  N  N  K  E  O  N  T
E  P  L  F  C  I  N  T  H  O  H
S  U  B  E  F  D  S  A  A  N  O
D  S  O  E  A  A  V  E  N  N  O
H  U  X  R  O  R  R  I  M  T  K
N  D  R  E  D  Y  E  G  A  R  S
```

ARTWORK	PENNANT
CALENDAR	PHOTO
CLOCK	POSTER
COAT HOOK	SCONCE
FLAG	SHELF
GRAFFITI	SIGN
INTERCOM	SPEAKER
MAILBOX	SPIDER-MAN
MAPS	SWITCH
MIRROR	THERMOSTAT

53. ONE-WORD MOVIE TITLES

```
O  I  H  C  C  O  N  I  P  R  J
A  I  A  I  O  I  M  S  O  U  U
D  G  L  N  D  B  I  B  M  A  B
L  Y  M  D  N  Y  M  A  M  S  F
I  A  A  E  M  A  N  U  A  O  I
T  L  B  R  L  J  Y  T  D  N  Y
A  H  I  E  I  R  N  L  E  I  I
M  I  E  L  E  O  D  B  L  D  A
N  U  S  L  H  T  A  A  I  O  C
T  H  L  A  O  L  H  E  N  R  P
T  O  C  A  T  O  H  O  E  P  L
A  O  B  O  N  N  Y  M  V  E  I
P  K  T  A  R  Z  A  N  N  E  O
U  R  H  O  B  M  E  F  M  O  N
F  L  U  B  B  E  R  V  I  E  S
```

ALADDIN	HEIDI
BABE	HOOK
BALTO	JUMANJI
BAMBI	MADELINE
BEETHOVEN	MATILDA
CINDERELLA	MULAN
DINOSAUR	PINOCCHIO
DUMBO	POCAHONTAS
FANTASIA	POLLYANNA
FLUBBER	TARZAN

54. ACTORS

```
T  H  E  F  I  S  R  S  T  N  N
A  M  E  O  F  D  I  E  F  O  I
S  P  A  C  E  Y  W  L  L  S  M
S  D  T  N  A  O  A  R  L  B  K
E  C  I  A  R  R  E  N  U  I  R
E  R  E  C  V  E  R  S  M  G  W
O  U  E  A  A  N  E  E  S  A  C
O  I  O  Y  L  P  G  G  Y  B  R
R  S  E  E  R  Z  R  A  A  E  O
V  E  P  H  O  E  N  I  X  C  E
R  S  L  T  B  S  N  H  O  E  M
O  K  U  L  N  P  T  N  F  A  I
N  N  H  T  I  M  S  S  O  I  N
H  A  A  T  W  T  A  I  R  C  I
W  H  T  N  E  M  S  O  D  A  N
```

CAGE	HANKS
CARREY	OSMENT
CONNERY	PHOENIX
CROWE	PITT
CRUISE	SMITH
DE NIRO	SPACEY
DICAPRIO	STILLER
FORD	WAHLBERG
GERE	WAYANS
GIBSON	WILLIS

55. ACTRESSES

```
A  V  M  A  M  P  P  I  R  E  A
C  T  R  I  E  A  D  N  O  F  S
B  S  T  U  L  R  R  I  N  S  D
H  A  R  T  O  A  A  W  A  N  A
L  N  R  O  E  Y  N  L  T  Z  O
F  O  R  R  E  L  I  O  L  O  L
W  S  W  L  Y  E  S  S  W  E  A
I  D  R  O  E  M  T  N  U  H  G
T  U  I  N  R  G  O  F  I  S  O
H  H  R  Y  F  D  N  R  Z  W  A
P  A  D  R  N  T  U  E  E  A  S
H  E  E  A  I  C  P  K  A  N  N
R  S  R  I  W  O  N  R  K  K  H
E  A  R  T  L  E  E  A  T  H  I
S  T  R  E  B  O  R  P  N  T  O
```

ANISTON	LOPEZ
BARRYMORE	MILANO
DIAZ	PALTROW
FONDA	PARKER
GELLAR	ROBERTS
HART	RYDER
HUDSON	SARANDON
HUNT	SWANK
HURLEY	WINFREY
KUDROW	WINSLET

56. IN THE LIBRARY

```
I  C  W  I  S  H  B  I  C  O  U
L  I  O  D  C  O  L  O  A  N  S
T  L  A  M  O  R  T  B  A  A  C
Q  B  F  K  P  K  C  I  I  N  S
C  U  S  R  I  U  R  I  H  O  S
O  P  I  L  E  A  T  I  S  M  D
E  C  N  E  R  E  F  E  R  U  R
B  M  E  B  T  T  N  O  R  E  M
N  O  I  T  C  I  F  H  S  E  A
L  L  A  T  Z  S  T  E  E  O  P
N  E  O  A  Y  U  A  T  V  O  S
F  T  G  H  A  R  T  L  L  I  B
C  A  R  D  C  E  O  R  E  A  R
M  Y  E  H  V  A  E  T  H  R  Y
N  I  G  V  I  D  E  O  S  H  T
```

BOOKS	MAPS
CARD	MUSIC
COMPUTER	PUBLIC
COPIER	QUIET
FICTION	READ
FORMS	REFERENCE
FREE	RESEARCH
LIBRARIAN	SHELVES
LOAN	STORY TIME
MAGAZINES	VIDEOS

14. GUESS THE THEME 1 WORD LIST

BURNT TOAST
CAVIAR
CHALKBOARD
COAL
COFFEE
CRUDE OIL
EBONY
EGGPLANT
INDIA INK
KARATE BELT

LABRADOR
NIGHT SKY
NUN'S HABIT
ONYX
PANTHER
PEPPER
RAVEN
SPIDER
SHADOW
TOP HAT

30. GUESS THE THEME 2 WORD LIST

AIRPLANE
BOOK
CALENDAR
CARDBOARD
CONFETTI
ENVELOPE
FILTER
KITE
LABEL
LUNCH BAG

MATCHES
MONEY
NAPKIN
ORIGAMI
POSTCARD
SPITBALL
STAMP
STATIONERY
STRAW
WASP NEST

38. GUESS THE THEME 3 WORD LIST

BENCH
BICYCLE
CHAISE
CHURCH PEW
CUSHION
HAMMOCK
HORSE
LOVE SEAT
MOTORCYCLE
OTTOMAN

RECLINER
ROCKER
SANTA'S LAP
SETTEE
SOFA
STOOL
SWING
THRONE
TOILET
TUFFET

44. GUESS THE THEME 4 WORD LIST

DAWN'S
EARLY
PROUDLY
HAILED
TWILIGHT'S
GLEAMING
STRIPES
STARS
PERILOUS
RAMPARTS

STREAMING
ROCKET'S
GLARE
BOMBS
BURSTING
FLAG
LAND
FREE
HOME
BRAVE

31. CROSSWORDSEARCH WORD LIST

BUTTER
CONSIDER
DOVE
FRENCH
GEENA
HASH
JINX
KITCHEN
LOSS
MAMMAL

NICKEL
PERSON
QUIT
RABBIT
SEVEN
TROUBLE
VAULT
WILLIAM
X-RAY
ZOOM

ANSWERS

1. SOUND OFF!

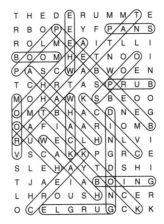

"The drummer boy from Illinois went crash, boom, bang": from Elvis Presley's hit "Jailhouse Rock."

2. UP AND DOWN, BACK AND FORTH

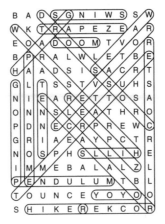

Basketball basics: "That's the way the ball bounces."

3. POP CHARTS 2001

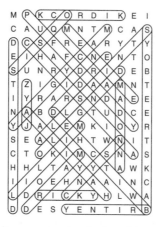

Me? I can't carry a tune in a bucket with two handles.

4. 21 MOST COMMON LAST NAMES

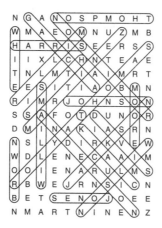

Name number sixteen, "Martin," is found inside name number nineteen, "Martinez."

5. HARRY POTTER

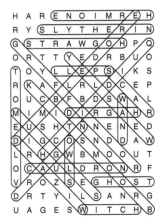

Harry Potter books are published in about forty languages.

6. CLASSIC TOYS

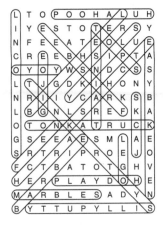

Toy Story featured Don Rickles as Mr. Potato Head.

7. "RUN ___"

A good dictionary will have well over one hundred definitions for "run."

8. POKÉMON

I will travel across the land, searching far and wide.

9. BOXING MATCH

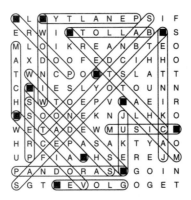

Life is like a box of chocolates: You never know what you are going to get.

10. HAPPY BIRTHDAY!

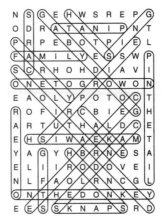

News report: People who have a lot of birthdays live longer.

11. IN THE GARDEN

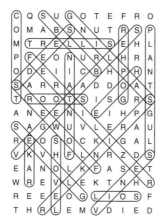

Quote from author Richard Diran: "I have a rock garden. Last week three of them died."

12. WEDDING BELLS

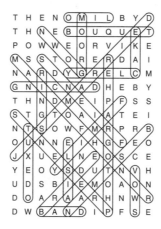

Then, by the power vested in me by this state, I now pronounce you husband and wife.

13. SCHOOL DAZE

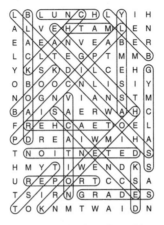

"I have never let my schooling interfere with my education."
—M[ark] Twain

14. GUESS THE THEME 1

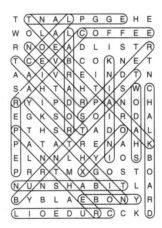

The word list contains things that are all or mostly black.

15. MONKEY BUSINESS

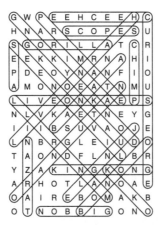

What kind of monkey is able to fly? A hot-air baboon!

16. ZZZZZZZZZZZZZZ

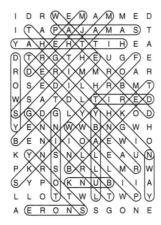

I dreamed I ate a huge marshmallow. When I woke up, my pillow was gone.

17. FINGER FUN

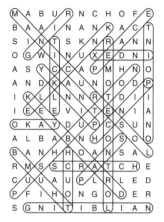

A bunch of bananas is known as a "hand," and individual bananas are called "fingers."

18. SMALL POTATOES

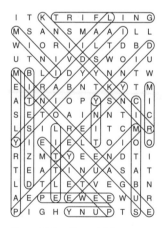

"It's a small world, but I wouldn't want to paint it."
—comedian Steven Wright

19. "HOW ARE YOU FEELING?"

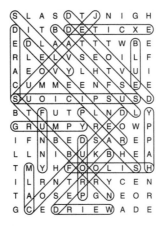

"Last night at twelve I felt immense, but now I feel like thirty cents."
—George Ade

20. GET A CLUE

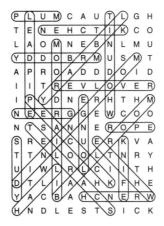

Caught! Colonel Mustard did it in the conservatory with the candlestick.

21. BRITISH-AMERICAN QUIZ

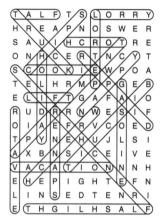

The answers are: one-c; two-a; three-g; four-e; five-j; six-b; seven-h; eight-f; nine-d; ten-i.

22. HORSEY SET

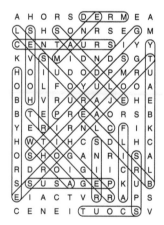

"A horse! a horse! my kingdom for a horse!"
—*Richard III*, act V, scene iv

23. LET'S EAT OUT TONIGHT

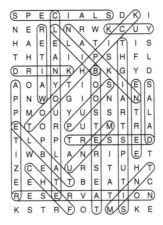

Diner: "What is this fly doing in my soup?" Waiter: "The backstroke."

24. SPORTS EQUIPMENT

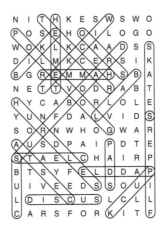

Nike's swoosh logo was designed by Carolyn Davidson, who was paid thirty-five dollars for it.

25. INANIMATE SPORTS TEAMS

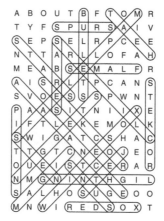

About forty-five percent of Americans own an item with a team logo on it.

26. SLOW DOWN!

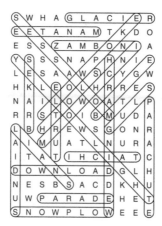

What does a snail say when it rides on a turtle's back? "Wheee!"

27. VALENTINE'S DAY

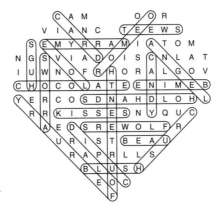

"Amor vincit omnia" is Latin for "Love conquers all."

28. THE PLAY'S THE THING

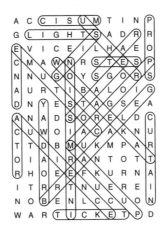

Acting advice: "Learn your lines and don't bump into the furniture."
—Noel Coward

29. JUST PLAIN MEAN

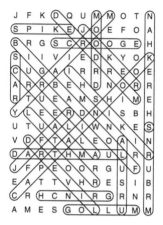

JFK quote: "Forgive your enemies, but never forget their names."

30. GUESS THE THEME 2

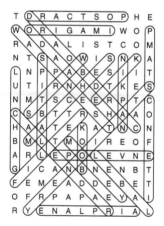

The word list contains items that are or can be made of paper.

31. CROSSWORDSEARCH

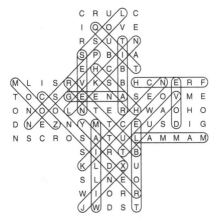

Cruciverbalist: someone who designs crosswords.

32. GET YOUR PAPER HERE!

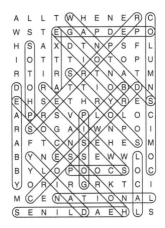

"All the News That's Fit to Print" is the slogan of *The New York Times*.

33. ART CLASS

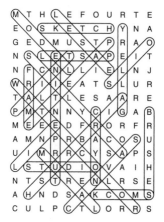

The four Teenage Mutant Ninja Turtles are named for famous painters and sculptors.

34. SNOW TIME

In the song, Frosty the Snowman has "a corncob pipe and a button nose and two eyes made out of coal."

35. GREETINGS FROM FLORIDA

The state song of Florida is Stephen Foster's "Old Folks at Home."

36. GOING BATTY

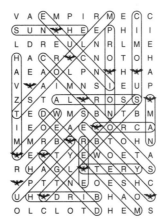

Vampire children learn the alpha-bat. In September they wear bat-to-school clothes.

37. TRIOS

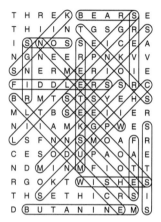

Three things I can never remember: names, faces, and I forgot the third.

38. GUESS THE THEME 3

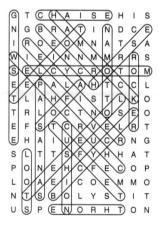

This grid contains all sorts of things that people commonly sit upon.

39. AW, NUTS!

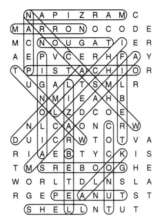

Coco-de-mer, a very rare coconut variety, is the world's largest nut.

40. EEEK!

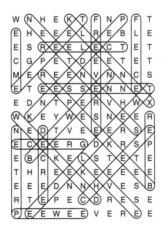

When the best get tested, they never rest. The keenest persevere!

41. SIX-LETTER WORLD CAPITALS

More world capital names begin with the letter "B" than any other, like Berlin and Beirut.

42. WAY TO GO!

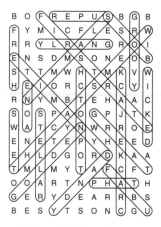

Bobby McFerrin's "Don't Worry, Be Happy" won the Grammy for the year's best song.

43. WHAT'S THAT ON YOUR HEAD?

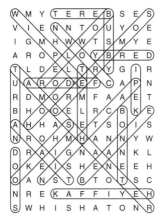

My seventy-eight-year-old grandfather has so many wrinkles he has to screw his hat on.

44. GUESS THE THEME 4

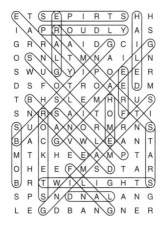

This grid contains words from the U.S. national anthem, "The Star-Spangled Banner."

45. YIDDISH WORDS

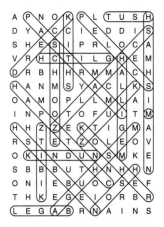

An old Yiddish proverb: "Many complain of their looks, but none of their brains."

46. JUST DUCKY

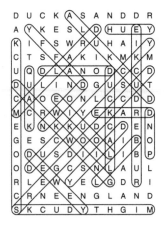

"Ducks and drakes" is what skimming stones is called in England.

47. GAS STATION SEARCH

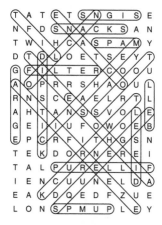

Attendant: "Why does your saucer have 'U.F.O.' printed on it?" Alien: "Unleaded Fuel Only."

48. BABY ANIMALS

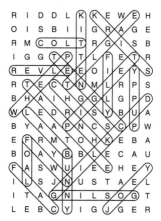

Riddle: Who is bigger, Mrs. Bigger or Mrs. Bigger's baby? Answer: The baby, because he is just a little Bigger!

49. A NUMBER OF THINGS

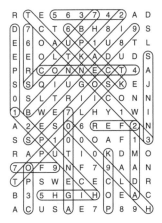

(Read this out loud) Question: Why was 6 so afraid of 7? Answer: Because 7 8 9!

50. LET THERE BE LIGHT

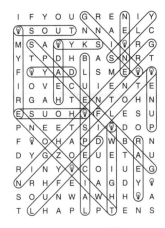

If you're in a car that's moving at the speed of light and you turn your headlights on, what happens?

51. SEVEN-LETTER GIRLS' NAMES

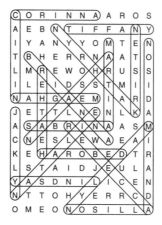

"A rose by any other name would smell as sweet," said Juliet to her Romeo.

52. WHAT'S THAT ON THE WALL?

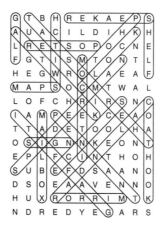

Building the Great Wall of China took one thousand seven hundred years.

53. ONE-WORD MOVIE TITLES

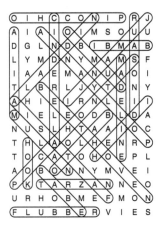

I'm so ugly my family hired an actor to play me in our home movies.

54. ACTORS

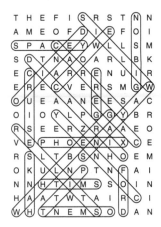

The first name of film star Keanu Reeves means "cool breeze over the mountains" in Hawaiian.

55. ACTRESSES

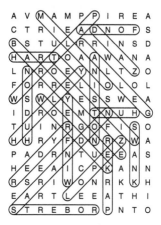

A vampire actress turns down a lot of roles waiting for a part she can sink her teeth into.

56. IN THE LIBRARY

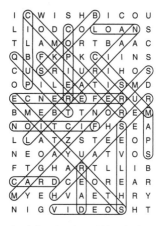

"I ... wish I could start back in school.... I'd be the last one out of that library every night." [—Malcolm X]

Index

Italics indicate answer page number

• • •

About the Author

JOHN CHANESKI is the author of *Super Party Games: Fun & Original Ideas for 10 or More.* An N.Y.U. graduate, he has parlayed a degree in drama into a strange career writing puzzles, articles, and reviews for various magazines. He has written trivia and designed games for several Web sites, and currently writes for a *very* popular TV game show. He lives in New York City with his wife, the poet Jennifer Michael Hecht.

WHAT IS MENSA?

Mensa
The High IQ Society

Mensa is the international society for people with a high IQ. We have more than 100,000 members in over 40 countries worldwide.

Anyone with an IQ score in the top two percent of population is eligible to become a member of Mensa—are you the "one in 50" we've been looking for?

Mensa membership offers an excellent range of benefits:
- Networking and social activities nationally and around the world;
- Special Interest Groups (hundreds of chances to pursue your hobbies and interests—from art to zoology!);
- Monthly International Journal, national magazines, and regional newsletters;
- Local meetings—from game challenges to food and drink;
- National and international weekend gatherings and conferences;
- Intellectually stimulating lectures and seminars;
- Access to the worldwide SIGHT network for travelers and hosts.

For more information about American Mensa:

www.us.mensa.org
Telephone: (800) 66-MENSA
American Mensa Ltd.
1229 Corporate Drive West
Arlington, TX 76006-6103
USA

For more information about British Mensa (UK and Ireland):

www.mensa.org.uk
Telephone:
+44 (0) 1902 772771
E-mail:
enquiries@mensa.org.uk
British Mensa Ltd.
St. John's House
St. John's Square
Wolverhampton WV2 4AH
United Kingdom

For more information about Mensa International:
www.mensa.org
Mensa International
15 The Ivories
6–8 Northampton Street
Islington, London N1 2HY
United Kingdom